THE FAT WOODWORKER

THE FAT WOODWORKER

BY
ANTONIO MANETTI

TRANSLATED WITH AN INTRODUCTION
AND NOTES BY
ROBERT L. MARTONE & VALERIE MARTONE

ITALICA PRESS
NEW YORK
1991

Copyright © 1991 by Robert L. Martone
and Valerie Martone

ITALICA PRESS, INC.
595 Main Street
New York, New York 10044

Library of Congress Cataloging-in-Publication Data

Manetti, Antonio, 1423-1497.
    [Novella del Grasso legnaiuolo. English]
    The fat woodworker / by Antonio Manetti : translated with
an introduction and notes by Robert L. Martone and Valerie Martone.
            p.   cm.
    Translation of : Novella del Grasso legnaiuolo.
    Includes bibliographical references.
    ISBN: 978-0-934977-23-4 (pbk.)   : $8.00
    1. Brunelleschi, Filippo, 1377-1446--Fiction. 2. Donatello,
1386?-1466--Fiction. I. Martone, Robert L., 1960-   . II.
Martone, Valerie, 1957-   .
III. Title.
PQ4627.M7N6813 1991
853'.2--dc20   90-55850
                                                                    CIP

Printed in the U.S.A. and E.U.
5 4 3

www.ItalicaPress.com

ABOUT THE TRANSLATORS

Valerie Martone received her Masters degree from Columbia University. She works as an editor. Robert L. Martone is a research scientist. Both received their undergraduate degrees from the State University of New York at Albany and have lived and studied in Italy. They are the editors and translators of *Renaissance Comic Tales of Love, Treachery, and Revenge,* also published by Italica Press.

CONTENTS

ILLUSTRATIONS

INTRODUCTION

THE FAT WOODWORKER is a delightful story in the tradition of the Italian Renaissance *beffe*, stories of practical, often cruel, jokes. It is the tale of a prank engineered by the great Renaissance architect, Filippo Brunelleschi (1377-1446), played upon an unsuspecting (and perhaps less-than-brilliant) woodworker named Manetto, in reprisal for the woodworker's social slight. While the prank is indeed cruel, it is so ingenious, and the victim is so comical, that the reader soon forgets the author's malice. The unfolding of the plot, at once amusing and frightening, is described by Mary McCarthy in *The Stones of Florence* as, "[A] picture of self alienation which is more terrifying and cleverer than anything in Pirandello." To the modern reader this story evokes the age of the Renaissance in Florence, where Brunelleschi, his friend Donatello, and their cohorts, are not imposing historical figures but, rather, playful, almost juvenile pranksters.

Florence, during the age of the Renaissance, was a thriving center of trade and industry, and its wealth was concentrated among a group of powerful merchant families that included the Strozzi, the Pitti, the Ruccellai, and the Medici. These wealthy families were patrons of a literary and artistic revival that included an emphasis upon classical learning. Cosimo de' Medici, for example, commissioned the translation of Plato's works from Marsilio Ficino. Cosimo gave Ficino a villa at Careggi where Ficino founded the Platonic Academy of Florence. The members of Ficino's Academy included many of the most important intellectual figures of the time, as well as members of the most prominent and powerful Florentine families, and his academy was the focal point of Renaissance Florentine humanism.

Along with scholarly and intellectual works, the secular literature of the age includes a number of humorous novellas, anecdotes, and stories that include the *beffe*. Popular in its own time, this humorous literature offers an intimate impression of the period.

Many examples of the *beffe* are found in Boccaccio's *Decameron,* in the *Tales of Firenzuola,* and in the works of lesser-known authors. A romantic twist to the usual trickery of the *beffe* is found in Gentile Sermini's *L'Inganno della Montanina.* Montanina is the wife of the jealous Andreoccio and the lover of the young and rich Vanino. In order to escape with her lover, Montanina takes a potent tranquilizer and, pretending to be near death, calls for a notary to take down her last wishes. She bequeaths everything to Andreoccio except a large case. The case is to be placed with her in her tomb, but its contents become the property of two Domenican brothers after the funeral. When the brothers open the case after her funeral and find Vanino inside, they run away in terror. Montanina awakens from the effects of her drug, and the two lovers flee to safety, leaving Andreoccio heartbroken over the death of his beautiful, young wife.

Sermini's novella is a direct antecedant of Shakespeare's *Romeo and Juliet*.

Lorenzo de' Medici's *Novella di Giacoppo* offers a more cynical approach to such romantic intrigues. Giacoppo is the old and jealous husband of Cassandra, a beautiful woman half his age. Francesco, a young student from another town and Cassandra's handsome lover, is afraid of being discovered by Giacoppo, so he devises a plan to safely enjoy Cassandra's company. Francesco employs Bartolomea, a woman of slight reputation from his hometown, to pretend to be his wife and, at the same time, to seduce Giacoppo. Bartolomea exhausts the old man's amorous energies until, one day, Bartolomea feigns repentance and convinces Giacoppo that he should go to a priest and confess his adultery. Giacoppo agrees and confesses his indiscretions to a priest who happens to be a friend of Francesco. The priest tells Giacoppo that by sleeping with Francesco's wife he has stolen Francesco's honor. The only way Giacoppo can save his soul and receive absolution for this horrible sin, he is told, is to get Francesco to sleep with Cassandra. Giacoppo asks Francesco for help in being pardoned by God, and for the love of God and the sake of his soul, Giacoppo begs Francesco to sleep with his wife. Francesco, feigning reluctance, agrees.

The Fat Woodworker is unique among these stories because it is the genre of the *beffe* distilled to its essence. In the story the Fat One provokes his friends by refusing their invitation to dinner. Deprived of the pleasure of his company at their gathering, his friends take the liberty of transforming him into another person. Here, the motive for the trick is not material or romantic gain, but simply the intellectual pleasure of the trick itself.

ℰↄ

THE AUTHOR of *The Fat Woodworker* is believed to be Antonio di Tuccio Manetti (1423-1497), a Florentine humanist and minor historical figure. He was a friend and companion of many artists and literary figures of his day and an admirer of Brunelleschi. A biography of Brunelleschi entitled *The Life of Filippo di Ser Brunellesco (Vita di Filippo di Ser Brunellesco)* is found in a collection of biographies of prominent Florentines, *Singular Men (Uomini Singholari),* which has also been attributed to Manetti. This biography is the principle source of information on Brunelleschi's life for Giorgio Vasari and other later biographers.

A member of a family of silk merchants, Manetti was vicar of Valdarno di Sopra and of Valdinievole, and he also held a number of high elective offices in the government of Florence. The executive branch of the Florentine government, called the Collegio, was made up of (in order of increasing importance) the Gonfaloniers of the greater guilds; the College of Bonomini, which was a group of twelve special advisors; and the Signoria, which was composed of eight Priors and the Gonfalonier of Justice. Manetti was one of the Bonomini in 1470, a Prior in 1476, and Gonfalonier of Justice in 1495. He was also Chief Magistrate of Colle di Val d'Elsa in 1496.

Because of his prominence and his knowledge of the arts and architecture, Manetti was selected as one of the

judges in the competition for the design of the facade of
Santa Maria del Fiore in 1490 (the original facade of the
cathedral of Florence, begun by Arnolfo di Cambio, was
never finished, and it was demolished in 1588).

Manetti had a wide range of interests, and, therefore,
he has been variously described by historians as a mathematician, astronomer, architect, copyist, neoplatonic
writer, Dante scholar, artist and dilettante. A glance at the
contents of the Zibaldone Manetti (Manetti miscellany),
a collection of manuscripts in Manetti's hand in the
National Library in Florence, reflects the variety of his
interests. The Zibaldone includes the astrological text, the
Book of the Archandreo by Gherardi di Cremona; a treatise
on the planets and stars; the geographical works, *Immago
Mundi* and *Della Imagine del Mondo di Santo Isidero;*
Filippo Villani's *De Origine Civitatis Florentiae;* a letter
from Francesco Petrarch to the community of Florence;
The Life of Charlemagne by Donato Acciaiuolo; and part
of a letter from Simone Botticelli to his brother Giovanni
(both of whom were brothers of the famous artist Sandro),
which included a report of spiritual apparitions in human
form in the forests of Bohemia.

Of particular interest among this collection are the
geographical works. Manetti's marginal annotations
indicate that he had discussed these texts with Paolo
del Pozzo Toscanelli (1397-1482), the mathematician and
physician who was a close friend of Brunelleschi, and who
would later play an essential role in launching Columbus
on his voyages of discovery. In 1474 Toscanelli wrote
to the Portugese King Alfonso V proposing a western
passage to the orient. Columbus was trying to enlist

royal patronage for an expedition across the Atlantic, and when he heard about Toscanelli's letter he wrote to the Florentine asking for more information. Toscanelli sent a map that Columbus would later carry to the New World. Manetti consulted with Toscanelli about matters that ultimately concerned the circumference of the world, an issue of great importance to any navigator contemplating a westward voyage to the orient.

Manetti is best known through the dedications and tributes of his more famous contemporaries. In *The Lives of the Artists* Vasari informs us that Paolo Uccello, obsessed with the artificial perspective invented by Brunelleschi, held long discussions on the subject of Euclidean geometry with Manetti. Uccello included Manetti among the five prominent Florentines whose portraits he kept in his house "to preserve their memory." Manetti represented achievement in mathematics. The others included Brunelleschi for achievement in architecture, Giotto for painting, Donatello for sculpture, and Uccello himself for perspective and animal painting.

Marsilio Ficino dedicated his vulgarization of both Dante's *De Monarchia* and his own *Commentarium in Convivium Platonis* (or *El Libro dello Amore*) to Manetti. Manetti had endeared himself to the Platonic Academy, and to Ficino in particular, by selecting and compiling the *dolce stil nuovo Rime* of the poet Guido Cavalcanti, and by dedicating the work to Cavalcanti's descendant Giovanni di Niccolo Cavalcanti, pupil of the "most learned platonist Marsilio Ficino."

While Ficino's dedications conferred great prestige upon Manetti, Girolamo Benivieni attributed to

Manetti a work that many believe to be Benivieni's very own. The work, entitled *Dialogues of Antonio Manetti, Citizen of Florence, on the Site, Form and Size of the Inferno of Dante* was dedicated to Manetti's brother Benedetto and was published in 1504, almost ten years after Manetti's death. The *Dialogues* are Benivieni's recollections of Manetti's observations on the *Inferno,* and the author uses Dante's descriptions of the light and shade at particular times of the day, the positon of the stars, and various other clues given by Dante to calculate the location, size, and form of the Inferno. (The site was calculated to be near the city of Cumae on the Bay of Naples.) A copy of Dante's *Commedia* in Manetti's hand, dated 1462, is found in the National Library in Florence, and it contains marginal notes and diagrams that similarly pertain to solar declinations and the positions of the stars in the *Commedia.* This indicates that Manetti had made the fundamental formulations of Benivieni's work, and this is confirmed by Cristoforo Landini's acknowledgement of the "work of our Antonio di Tuccio Manetti" in his edition of the *Commedia* published in 1481, which contained a commentary appropriately called *Site, Form and Measure of the Inferno and the Height of the Giants and of Lucifer.* The essential arguments of the *Dialogues* would later be supported by Galileo.

Manetti is sometimes confused, for obvious reasons, with Antonio Manetti (d. 1461), called Ciaccheri, an assistant to Brunelleschi. Ciaccheri was a woodworker who made Brunelleschi's wooden architectural models, and he was involved in the actual construction of many of Brunelleschi's buildings. When Ciaccheri made a model for Brunelleschi's design of the cathedral lantern for the competition in 1425, he entered his own design in direct competition with his master. Tuccio Manetti attacked Ciaccheri for this and considered it presumptuous of the woodworker to try to outdo the great architect. Tuccio Manetti also accused Ciaccheri of ruining his master's work by incompetence and by acts of deliberate sabotage. For these reasons, Ciaccheri, or this other Manetti, was believed by some to be the Manetto of this story. Most, however, believe that the victim was Manetto di Jacopo Ammannatini (d. 1450), called Manetto of Florence, a worker in intarsia, since the details of his life closely match those of the story. According to tradition, the events of this story actually took place.

℘

THE FAT WOODWORKER is very much a celebration of the genius of Filippo di Ser Brunellesco, the architect credited with reviving the classical aesthetic. To quote McCarthy again, "This genius [of Brunelleschi], which found the way to calculate the vanishing point, could make a bulky man [The Fat] vanish or seem to himself to vanish, like a ball juggled by a conjurer while still in plain sight." McCarthy's synopsis of the story's point is apropos because Brunelleschi's most influential achievement was the invention of artificial perspective. This is a method for determining and accurately representing the size of an object, or part of an object, in proportion to its distance from a point of observation. The use of Brunelleschi's invention in a two-dimensional painting gives the illusion of a third dimension, or depth. Before the invention of artificial perspective, proportions were relative to the importance of the figure (the more important figures being larger than the less important figures, regardless of their spatial arrangement), or they were determined intuitively. It is generally agreed that Brunelleschi invented this method between 1413 and 1420, before undertaking any of his major architectural works.

Brunelleschi's method is called "artificial" perspective in order to distinguish it from "natural" perspective, the general term for the medieval study of optics and vision. Works on natural perspective were widely read, and Chaucer refers to the authorities on this subject in "The Squire's Tale":

And somme of hem wondred on the mirour,
That born was up into the maister-tour,
Hou men myghte in it swiche thynges se.
Another answerde, and seyde it myghte wel
Naturelly, by composiciouns
Of anglis and of slye reflexiouns,
And seyde that in Rome was swich oon
They speken of Alocen (Alhazan), and Vitulon
   (Witelo),
And Aristotle, that writen in hir lyves
Of queynte mirours and of perspectives,
As knowen they that han hir bookes herd.

There has been considerable speculation about specific sources that might have inspired Brunelleschi's invention. His use of a mirror to view one of his perspective paintings suggests that he had these authorities on natural perspective in mind, particularly as they referred to reflected images in mirrors. Vitruvius made some scant reference to a method in his *Ten Books on Architecture;* and while some have suggested that this work led to the invention, the first certain reference to Vitruvius' work is by Poggio Bracciolini in 1415. It is not certain that Brunelleschi had timely access to this work. Also, much emphasis has been placed upon Brunelleschi's forty-year friendship with Paolo del Pozzo Toscanelli, who gave him lessons in geometry, and who is known to have provided the Florentine artists with a work on perspective, *Quaestiones Perspectivae,* by the Paduan mathematician, Bagio Pelacani. However, it seems that Toscanelli provided the lessons in geometry and the source on perspective after Brunelleschi made his invention. Toscanelli only returned from his studies in Padua in 1425, and in 1413, the earliest date given to Brunelleschi's invention, Toscanelli was only sixteen years old. In his biography of Brunelleschi, Manetti dismisses the usefulness of any earlier sources for this invention by stating that the few remaining documents from the ancients on this subject were unintelligible. In *The Life of Brunelleschi* Manetti describes at length two paintings made by Brunelleschi that demonstrate his method.

The artificial perspective had a far greater significance to the Renaissance mind than mere accuracy or realism in painting and sculpture. The stunning beauty of Renaissance art is due in part to realism, but more importantly to a classical aesthetic of harmony and balance. The mathematical method of artificial perspective, in which all points in space are considered equivalent, is a reflection of this aesthetic. The method of artificial perspective validated the perception of the senses and defined those perceptions in mathematical terms, and the mathematical basis of the method was direct evidence that nature itself was rational and could be understood in rational terms. Finally, because this method was a subject of learned speculation, it elevated the profession of the artist to a learned profession.

℃

IF THE INVENTION of the artificial perspective is Brunelleschi's greatest intellectual work, his greatest substantial work is the cupola of Santa Maria del Fiore, the cathedral of Florence. Vasari states that Brunelleschi "made the joke about the Fat Man and Matteo" while busy designing this cupola. Construction of Santa Maria del Fiore began in 1294. The cathedral was built on an optimistic, if not arrogant, scale, apparently with little concern over the technical details involved in raising a stone cupola measuring 140 feet across with a base rising 180 feet above the ground. In 1412 construction of the cathedral was nearing completion, and a plan for raising the cupola was desperately needed.

Domes were typically built at that time by spanning the opening of the roof with wooden crossbeams and raising a wooden framework to support and center the stones of the dome until the keystone was inserted and the structure became self-supporting. However, no trees could be found that were long enough to span the opening at the base of the dome, and even if such timber could have been found, it would certainly have been crushed under the weight of a stone dome of this size. The complexity of the problem was such that one serious proposal envisioned filling the cathedral with earth to the 180-foot base of the cupola, and erecting a wooden framework on the earthen fill. An indication of the enormous scale of the project is given by the fact that once construction of the cupola was underway, a complete canteen was set up on the scaffolding at the work site because workers were wasting too much time climbing to and from their work for their lunch. The size of the cathedral, no doubt intended to be a focus of Florentine civic pride, could easily have become a point of humiliation if a solution could not be found.

It was well known that Brunelleschi spent a great deal of time and effort in Rome, excavating and detailing classical ruins with his close friend Donatello. Manetti credits Brunelleschi's knowledge of Roman antiquities for the solutions to some of the problems posed by the construction of this cupola.

Brunelleschi's solution was a double shelled dome of light stone and brick whose weight is carried by a stone ribbing. This hollow double shell dome is much lighter than a solid stone structure would have been. The entire structure was self-supporting during construction: each horizontal course of the dome was able to support its own weight and the weight of the next course of stone being laid upon it. Because of this, no wooden framework was required to build or center the dome. This double shell dome and its manner of construction was later imitated by Michaelangelo and Giacomo della Porta in the design and construction of Saint Peter's Basilica in Rome.

Brunelleschi shared the commission for the construction of the cupola with Lorenzo Ghiberti (1378-1455), a man with whom he had a less-than-amicable relationship. This relationship reveals much about Brunelleschi's character and Manetti's partisanship.

Ghiberti was a renowned sculptor and architect, and he was the author of the *Commentarii,* an autobiography as well as a history and a treatise on art. He is best known for the sculpted bronze doors of the Florentine Baptistery, christened by Michaelangelo, "The Gates of Paradise." The rivalry between Brunelleschi and Ghiberti dates to the competition for the design of these doors.

According to Vasari, Brunelleschi withdrew his entry from the competition once he saw Ghiberti's brilliantly executed entry. But Manetti tells a very different story. According to Manetti, all of the entrants in the competition worked diligently and, except for Ghiberti, they worked in secret. Ghiberti constantly sought out the opinions, sugestions and advice of the judges of the competition, and he tried to find out as much as he could about Brunelleschi's entry. The judges, according to Manetti, could not but look favorably upon Ghiberti's execution of their own advice. Nor could they ignore the beauty of Brunelleschi's entry. As a result, they offered a joint commission to Brunelleschi and Ghiberti, which Brunelleschi declined.

With the exception of Vasari – who drew from both Manetti and Ghiberti's *Commentarii* – public opinion of Ghiberti declined from Manetti's rather low opinion.

The manuscript known as *Anonimo Magliabecchiano* (c.1505) stressed the help of Donatello, Luca della Robbia, and Brunelleschi himself in the completion of the doors. Later art historians transformed Ghiberti's assistants into collaborators, and each subsequent historian lengthened the list of collaborators, diminishing Ghiberti's role in his own masterpiece with each additional name.

Nor did Brunelleschi have a sterling reputation when he began work on the dome of the cathedral. He became frustrated while trying to win the commission for the construction of the cupola and proposed that the commission should be awarded to the architect who could make an egg stand on end. Eggs were obtained and after several people tried and failed, Brunelleschi took an egg and smashed it on end. And when Brunelleschi flew into a rage after one of his proposals for this same project was rejected, those present thought that he was deranged and had him physically carried away. According to Vasari, Brunelleschi was given a partner in his commission for the cupola "to restrain (his) impetuosity." Much to his despair, the person chosen to be his partner was Ghiberti.

Brunelleschi was consoled by his friends Donatello and Luca della Robbia, and he accepted the joint commission as equally determined, it seems, to discredit Ghiberti as to show himself equal to the demands of the project. Brunelleschi feigned illness at critical times during the construction of the cupola to force Ghiberti to take charge. When Ghiberti refused to take any action alone, Brunelleschi, having exposed Ghiberti's uncertainty and incompetence, complained that Ghiberti was capable only of collecting his salary. At other times, Brunelleschi had different aspects of the project divided absolutely between them; this allowed Brunelleschi to complain vehemently over the manner in which Ghiberti completed his part of the work, and it gave him the opportunity to explain how he could easily have done the work better than Ghiberti.

These accounts of Brunelleschi's behavior led the psychologist Michael Kubovy to diagnose Brunelleschi as "[an] extraordinarily ambitious, competitive, secretive, slightly paranoid, cunning, somewhat manipulative genius." Manetti's praise of Brunelleschi in *The Fat Woodworker* is neither so reluctant nor so pejorative. In the story, when Brunelleschi's friends gather after the plot is complete to marvel at the delicate interplay of the plot with fate, it is clear that Brunelleschi is the divine architect of that fate.

ඏ

WHAT IS PERHAPS MOST UNIQUE about *The Fat Woodworker* is the author's emphasis upon the victim's psychology and his sense of self. Much of the action, indeed much of the humor, of the story is found not in the interactions between the characters, but in the narration of Manetto's thoughts. The reader follows Manetto with delight as he at first insists that he is who he has always been, then as he relents into thinking that he has become somebody else, and finally as he returns to thinking of himself again as Manetto, only to worry that he has perhaps become yet another person.

The story's focus upon the sense of self epitomizes what Burkhart termed "the Renaissance discovery of the individual," a discovery he considered central to the character of Renaissance culture. In *The Civilization of the Renaissance in Italy*, Burkhart cited the use of terms, such as "singular men" (as in Manetti's *Uomini Singholari*) and indeed the growth of historical biography as reflecting an awareness in the Renaissance of a person's uniqueness and individuality, rather than his definition by social class or profession.

Burkhart states that "the corrective... of all highly developed individuality is found in ridicule, especially when expressed in the victorious form of wit," so it is not ironic that this story, which is so focused upon the concept of the singularity of the person, steals this exact sense from its central character. Manetto's singularity is the precise reason he is singled out to be the victim of this plot.

೧

MANETTI'S TALE contains a number of classical references that are, for the most part, poorly developed. Perhaps the most relevant reference is to Apuleius' *The Golden Ass*. In his commentary on *The Golden Ass* Beroaldus (c.1505) states that "[Apuleius] conveyed the lessons of palingenesis and metempsychosis, that is, of regeneration and transmutation, through the disguise of [a] ludicrous story." Apuleius' story is one of initiation into the divine mysteries that involves the loss of the self. In *The Fat Woodworker*, Manetto also loses himself in an absurd chain of events and finds himself tied into a knot that "Aristotle himself could not untie." But Manetto's reward is worldly rather than divine, and the only hint of revelation is "the greatest laugh of all" had and kept secret by the Fat One.

It is fitting that Manetto should receive such a mundane reward for all his trouble because, throughout the story Manetto is as concerned with losing his possessions as with losing his mind. Manetto is called "The Fat" *(Il Grasso),* and like the "Fat Men" *(I Grassi)* he resembles, "Fat" does not refer simply to obesity, but rather to the "Popoli Grassi," as the comfortable Florentine middle class was called.

While Manetti has given us this story to express his extreme admiration for Brunelleschi, it is unlikely that he is the original author of *The Fat Woodworker.* A shorter version of the same story, which ends abruptly when the Fat One regains his own identity, and which is devoid of any classical reference, has been attributed to an unknown author of the first half of the fifteenth century. The reference to Apuleius (first published in 1469) dates Manetti's version of this story to the second half of the same century. Manetti himself makes reference to an earlier author who "did well to keep the story from being totally lost." Manetti also has done well to leave us his wonderfully embellished version of this story for our complete enjoyment. ❧❧❧

THE FAT WOODWORKER

THE CITY OF FLORENCE has had some very
pleasant and amusing fellows in times past, and this is
especially true of recent times as, when in the year 1409,
a certain group of honorable men found themselves
together one night at dinner. This was a group composed
of men dedicated to the public life: some were master
artisans and craftsmen, some were painters, some were
goldsmiths, some were sculptors, some woodworkers
and other types of artisans. They gathered together at
the home of Tomaso Pecori, a very pleasant and upright
man of intellect. He was drawn to their intelligence and
skill and took great pleasure in their company.

Once they had dined cheerfully, they sat together
here and there in small groups near the fire, because
it was winter, and they discussed various and pleasant
things and conferred among themselves upon the highest
aspects of their arts and professions. While they were
chatting together one of them asked, "Why is it that
Manetto the woodworker is not here tonight?" Since he
had only one name, Manetto was often called the "Fat
One." It became clear from what was said that some of
the group had seen Manetto but, for whatever reason,
none had been able to bring him along.

I

The woodworker had his workshop near Piazza di San Giovanni and was at the time one of the best masters of his art in Florence. Among other things he was famous for making devotional tables, altar tables, and other such things that not just any woodcarver could make. He was a wonderful person, as were most fat men. He was about twenty-eight years of age, and he was large and robust; and for this reason he came to be known by one and all as the "Fat One."

He was actually a bit simple, but he wasn't so very simple that anyone other than a very shrewd person would perceive his simplicity. Manetto the Fat was always in the habit of being with this group, and the reason for his absence that night became a subject of great speculation. But, not finding a reason, they concluded that nothing other than some sort of caprice on his part would have prevented him from coming.

Because they felt a little bit scorned by him – since almost all of them were of better position and quality than he was – they merrily contemplated how they might avenge this injury. The person who spoke first said, "If only we could play a joke on him and make it discreet enough so that it could be saved for a second time."

One of the others responded, "If only we could play a trick on him so that he would pay for our dinner without being here himself!"

Among the fellows of the group was Filippo di Ser Brunellesco, a man of marvelous genius and intellect, as most people already knew. He was at that time about thirty-two years old, and he was on familiar terms with Manetto and knew him well and fondly and sometimes discreetly asked favors of him. Considering this, Filippo was somewhat upset and said, "I would give my heart if we could play a nice joke for our revenge on the one who did not attend tonight, on the condition that it will give us great pleasure and amusement. If you do not believe that we can do this successfully, I will give you my heart. This is what I think: We can make him believe that he has become another person, and that he is no longer Manetto the Fat." He said this with a certain sardonic grin that demonstrated his great self-confidence. Once again the group recognized Filippo to be a great genius – how sad is the blind man who cannot see the sun – and knew he would devote his brilliance to this prank, since he made those things that he labored at turn out so intelligently.

However, it happened that not everyone in the group knew of Manetto's simplicity, and those people judged the prank to be totally impossible. But, as someone who is very capable, Filippo exposed his subtle and cautious reasonings and with an elaborate discussion he convinced them that the plot could succeed. While in agreement that the plan would have to be kept secret, they concluded with great amusement that the vendetta would be carried out. Manetto the Fat would be convinced that he had become someone called Matteo, whom both they and Manetto knew, but he was not one of those intimates who gathered together to dine with one another. They made this agreement with the greatest laugh in the world and felt so much better and so happy that some of them broke into song.

ᘒ

THE HERO OF THIS PLEASANT STORY would not wait. Rather, on the following night, Filippo – who knew the Fat One as well as himself – went to Manetto's shop at the hour of dusk, when it was usual to lock up all the shops for this type of work. (As a friend, Manetto confided everything in Filippo, otherwise Filippo would not have been able to do what he planned.) There he met Manetto, where he had found him a thousand other times at that hour. They were in the middle of dis-cussing something when, as planned, a small boy arrived.

The boy, appearing very distressed, asked, "Are you here, Filippo di Ser Brunellesco?"

At this, Filippo stepped in front of the boy and said, "Yes, here I am. What do you want?"

The boy responded, "If you are who you say you are, go to your house at once."

Filippo said, "God help me! What has happened?"

The boy answered, "I was sent to find you, and the reason is that two hours ago your mother had a serious accident, and she is nearly dead. This is why you must go to her at once."

Filippo expressed great disbelief when he heard this, recommended himself to God once again, and grabbed hold of Manetto. As one would speak to a friend Manetto said, "I want to go with you in case you need me to do something or other. These are not circumstances in which one wants to leave a person alone. I want to lock up the shop and go with you."

Filippo in gratitude said, "I don't want you to come right now. We cannot be certain that this thing is very important. But if I should need anything, I will let you know. Wait for me in your shop for a little while and don't leave for any reason. Then, if I don't send any message after a while, go on your way."

Filippo left, leaving the Fat One at the shop and, pretending to go to his own house, he went secretly to the Fat One's house, which was near Santa Maria del Fiore.

Filippo expertly opened the lock with a knife – as one who knows how – entered the house and locked himself in, bolting the door shut so that no one else could enter. Now, the Fat One had a mother, but she was away in a villa in Polverosa for several days to do laundry, and to salt meat, and to do many other things that the Fat One needed. From time to time she would return, as the Fat One thought necessary, and enter the house using a knife. This was the reason the door was left as it was – so it could be opened with a knife – and Filippo knew it.

Manetto worked a little bit in his shop, and then more deliberately to satisfy his promise to Filippo, he paced back and forth many times inside the shop, and after a while he said, "Things must not have gone badly with Filippo, and he doesn't need me." With these words he locked his shop, started toward his house, and arrived at its entrance.

The entrance to Manetto's house has two great staircases. Manetto climbed the stairs and tried to open the door in his usual way but, after trying several times, he was unable to open it. He realized that the door was locked from inside, and, pounding hard on the door, he shouted, "Who's in there? Open up." He guessed that his mother had returned and locked the door for some precaution, and she didn't hear the knocking.

Meanwhile, Filippo placed himself at the head of the stairs, and mimicking the shouts of the Fat One – whom he wanted to imitate completely – shouted, "Who's out there?"

Manetto recognized that the person inside was someone other than his mother and said, "I am Manetto the Fat."

To this Filippo pretended that the one he heard was that Matteo whom they wanted Manetto to believe he had become. Filippo said, "Beh! Matteo, go on. I have had a mountain of troubles today. Not long ago, Filippo di Ser Brunellesco was at my shop. He had come to tell me how his mother, a few hours before, was in danger of death. That is why I have had a bad night." Filippo turned around and, pretending to speak to his mother, said, "Do as I say. In two days you'll have to return and return at night as well." And with a good many words he scolded his mother.

Manetto listened to the person in the house scold his mother like this, and that person seemed to him to have not only his – Manetto's – own voice but all his habits; and he said, "What can I say to this? It seems to me that whoever is in there is me. He said that Filippo was in his shop as he was with me, and as with me he had come to say that his mother was ill. And besides that, he shouts like a youth and has my way of speaking. Could I be so absent minded…?"

He went down the two large staircases and turned around to call up to the windows when, as planned,

Donatello the sculptor – whose greatness is well-known to all – arrived. Donatello was among the group at dinner and was Manetto's friend. Arriving like this at dusk, he said, "Good evening Matteo. Are you looking for Manetto the Fat? He has only been home for a little while. He didn't stop to greet anyone but just dragged himself home."

The Fat One was astonished to hear these things. He was even more astonished than ever to hear Donatello call him Matteo. He was overcome with confusion, and he tensed and turned to face Piazza di San Giovanni, thinking, "I have been here many times before, so I should meet someone who knows me and can tell me who I am." He continued, "Alas! Unhappy me! Could I ever have been such a simpleton that I could so quickly be turned into someone else without my ever knowing it?"

While Manetto was in the piazza, six agents of the office of the Mercatánzia gathered in the distance as planned. Among the agents was a messenger and a man who pretended to be a creditor of Matteo, whom the Fat One had begun to believe himself to be. They accosted the Fat One, and the one who pretended to be the creditor said, "Wait. This is my debtor. He knows that I have been searching for him and that now I have finally picked him out."

The soldiers took hold of Manetto and began to lead him away. The Fat One turned to the one who had ordered him arrested, planted his feet and said, "What have I done to you that you are having me arrested? What have I gotten myself into? You have taken me by mistake… I am not who you think I am. And you do me a great villainy to disgrace me like this, since I have done nothing to you! I am Manetto the Fat, the woodworker, and I am not Matteo, and I do not know this Matteo of whom you speak."

He wanted to strike out at them since he was large and strong, but they quickly grabbed his arms while the creditor stood in front of him and said, "What do you mean you don't know me and you have nothing to do with me? What! Don't I know my debtors? And who is this Manetto the Fat, the woodworker? I have you written in my book of debtors, and it is a good thing that I hadn't sentenced you a year ago or more. What do you mean, you have nothing to do with me? And you also say that you are not Matteo. The rogue! Take him away! This time you will have to meet payments before you're let go. We will see what name you will be called then."

And so, quarreling among themselves, they led him to prison. And because it was half an hour before eight o'clock and suppertime, and because it was dark already, they didn't meet anyone on their way who would know him.

When they arrived the notary stopped to write the name of Matteo in the book of the debtors' prison. The notary put Manetto into prison and went off to tell Tomaso Pecori of all that had happened, since Tomaso and the notary were close friends.

The other prisoners who were there heard the uproar when Manetto arrived and heard him called Matteo. Therefore, they welcomed him many times as Matteo, and they called him by this name, which they overheard, as they would often do without asking any further. By chance there was no one there in the prison who knew him, at least by sight. And because he was called Matteo by all of them, he became almost certain that he appeared to be another person.

When he was asked why he was being held, he said, "I have to give a great deal of money to someone, so I am here. But I will get out very early tomorrow morning."

One of the prisoners said, "You see, we are having dinner. Dine with us, and then tomorrow morning you will be free. But we are warning you well that one always stays here a bit longer than one would otherwise believe. Give thanks to God so that no one will interfere with your release."

The Fat One accepted his invitation to dine in this dirty hovel and ate some of the scraps that one of the prisoners gave him. One of them said, "Matteo, make yourself as comfortable as you can tonight, and tomorrow morning, if you get out, well done. But if not, send for some clothes from your home."

The Fat One thanked him and prepared to go to sleep as best he could. Meanwhile, once he had accomplished his task at the prison, the young man who played the role of the creditor went off to meet with Filippo di Ser Brunellesco to tell him every detail of the tribulation of the Fat One and of his arrest.

The Fat One settled into a corner of his cell and began to worry, saying to no one in particular, "What must I do if I've become Matteo? It seems to be certain now, since there could never be so many signs as I have seen, all of them agreeing that I am Matteo, and it not be true. But what Matteo is this? And if I happen to send home to my mother for clothes and the Fat One is there in the house, what would they think of it? If it is true, they will make a joke of me."

The Fat One was left with these thoughts, affirming himself first to be Matteo, and then Manetto, until the morning. He got almost no sleep, but only naps whose dreams tormented him with all their controversies. He got up like the others and stood at the small window of the prison exit, hoping to happen by chance upon someone who knew him and who might help him escape from the torment that he had begun to feel that night.

Giovanni di Messer Francesco Rucellai entered the Mercatánzia at that time. He was part of that company at dinner and was part of the pleasant conspiracy. He knew the Fat One well and, in fact, Manetto was making a devotional table to Our Lady for him at that time; he spoke with Manetto the day before for a long time at his shop to urge Manetto to finish. Manetto had promised to give him the finished devotional table in four days.

This fellow arrived at the Mercatánzia and stepped up to the prison window, which was then on the first floor, where the Fat One stood.

Manetto saw Giovanni and watched him with a knowing and familiar smile. Giovanni saw his expression, and looking at him as if he had never seen him before, because he did not know Matteo, said, "What are you smiling about, friend?"

The Fat One answered, "No… about nothing." Seeing that Giovanni didn't recognize him, he asked, "Good man, do you know of a man who is known as the

Fat One, who works as a woodworker around the corner from Piazza di San Giovanni? Tell me."

Giovanni said, "Of course! Yes, I know him very well. He is a good friend of mine, and soon I will go to him to pick up a little bit of work that he has done for me. Has he put you here in your cell?"

The Fat One said, "No, Holy Mary!" And then, "Forgive me, but I must ask something of you in confidence. For pity's sake do me a favor since you have to go to him for other reasons anyway. For pity's sake tell him that one of his friends is being held in the prison at the Mercatánzia and says that he would like to have a word with him, if he could pass by for a minute."

Giovanni, looking him in the eye and restraining his urge to laugh with great effort said, "Who are you that I should say sent for him?" (He asked this so that Manetto would confess to being Matteo and to add more weariness to his problems.)

The Fat One said, "Never mind. It is enough for you to tell him this."

Giovanni said, "I will do it with pleasure, if you think it suffices."

Giovanni left and found Filippo, informing him, with great laughter, of everything.

The Fat One stayed by the window of the prison saying to himself, "Now at last I can be certain that I am no longer the Fat One. Oh! Giovanni Rucellai didn't even raise his eyes to me. He didn't know me as the one who is at the workshop at every hour, and he doesn't forget people either! I am no longer the Fat One, this is certain, and I have become Matteo. What I am told is my destiny and my disgrace. What if this fact was betrayed? I would be reviled and considered crazy, and children would run away from me. I will have to endure many perils. Besides this, what will I do with the debts of someone else, and what of the intrigues and of the thousand other errors that I have always watched out for and that could put me in danger? Besides this, one cannot discuss this thing with anyone else; one cannot take counsel on this! And God only knows that I need it! I am troubled in every way. We will see if the Fat One comes, and if he does I will understand, perhaps, what this all means. Could it be that he has become me?"

And so, he waited a good long time with great hope for the Fat One to arrive. And when he did not come, Manetto moved back from the window to give space to someone else. He looked now at the floor and at the cell walls, the fingers of his hands in knots.

It was on that day in this prison that a judge was detained for a debt. He was a very skilled man who was famous for his writing and learning, and for this reason his name will be kept secret. Because of this fellow's high position he didn't know the Fat One, but when he saw Manetto so melancholy and with an air of such great sadness, he then wanted to know him. The judge thought the Fat One was in such a state because of a debt of a grave nature, such as had fixed his own case. He didn't want him to worry so, and since he would leave there soon he tried to comfort the Fat One for charity's sake (as he did every so often) by saying, "Listen! Matteo, you are so melancholy, it is as if you might soon die or you are in danger of some great disgrace. Don't worry any more.

According to what you say, this is a small debt. One shouldn't be so discouraged by one's fortunes. Why haven't you sent for some friend or relative? Have you no one? Ah, try to pay your debt or make an agreement in some way so that you can leave prison, and don't give yourself to such sadness."

Finding himself comforted with such courtesy and such kind words, he didn't tell the judge that he had, perhaps, become someone else.

"And why is it that you don't want to tend to your business?"

The Fat One, knowing the judge to be a good man, decided to speak with him while he was still there and, with every reverence to the judge, to entirely open his case to him for his intervention.

So, turning to him from one corner of the prison cell, the Fat One said to him, "Sir, I know that you don't know me, but I know you well, and I know that you are a valiant man. The kindness you have shown me and the benevolence that is your custom gives me reason, as I have decided, to tell you what makes me so melancholy. I don't want you or anyone else to believe that I would be so sad over such a small debt, because even without this debt I would still be a poor artisan with much grief. Rather, it is for another reason that I am like this, and it is something that, in truth, has great importance to me. It is, perhaps, something that has never before happened to anyone in the world."

Hearing this, the judge was quite astonished. He sat up straight to listen with great attention.

The Fat One started from the beginning and toward the end of telling what he had endured with great fatigue, he tried to conceal his tears. He pleaded with the judge to tell him specifically two things. First, he asked how a person such as himself could ever speak for his own honor. Second, he asked the judge if he could offer any counsel or remedy.

He said, "Sir! I know that you have read widely of many things and many stories of the ancients and of the present and of men that have written upon facts and events. Have you ever come across a similar thing?"

When the valiant man heard this fellow, he quickly considered the situation and imagined that it was due to one of two possible causes. This fellow had either lost his senses because of some great melancholy or because of his present debt (as might a man of little spirit), or that truly this fat man was playing a joke upon him.

In order to understand better, the judge responded that he had read much about it, that is, about being changed from one person into another and that it was not a new thing. "Not only that, worse things have happened. There were those who were changed into brute animals, like Apuleius who became an ass, and Actaeon who became a stag. One can read of many others that I do not recall right now." He said this as one who was trying to get himself out of trouble, because he was speaking off the cuff.

At this the Fat One said, "Oh! I would never have believed this. But you have given me faith that this is the truth, because everything you say is the truth." Then he added, "Now tell me. If I who was the Fat One am changed into Matteo, what has become of *him*?"

The judge responded, "He has changed into the Fat One. This is a reciprocal case. It is like a pair of shoes. From what I have read and from what I have seen here, it is quite amazing. I suppose you want me to visit this fellow for a bit?"

"This really is something to laugh about so long as you are not in the middle of it, as I certainly am!" said the Fat One.

"Exactly," answered the judge. "These are great misfortunes, and may God watch over every man. We are all under this threat. I had a worker to whom this same thing just happened."

The Fat One sighed heavily, and he didn't know what more he could say.

The judge added, "One can read of similar things with the companions of Ulysses and with the other transmutants of Circe. It is the truth, from all that I have heard and read. If I remember well, some of them have just returned. But, occasionally it happens that the event lasts longer, if indeed it ever resolves itself at all." He said this to put the Fat One into more confusion.

The Fat One was amazed to hear this. By this time it was almost nine o'clock and he hadn't yet eaten. The two brothers of this Matteo now came to the Mercatánzia. They asked the notary at the desk if one of their brothers who was named Matteo was being held there, and for how much he was being held, because they wanted to release him from prison.

The notary said, "Yes," and pretended to search for his name in his book. After many turns of the pages he said, "It is for a lot." And he told them the name of the person who made the petition.

"It is too much," one of them said. Then they said, "We wish to speak with him for a little while," and after that they said they would give the order to pay for him.

At the prison they spoke to one of the prisoners who was near the bars: "Go over there and tell Matteo that his two brothers are here and that he should come over here and speak with them for a minute."

When the brothers looked into the cell they recognized the judge who, by chance, had been speaking with the Fat One, and they knew him very well.

The Fat One was made very sad and troubled by what the judge had told him, and he asked him what had happened to his worker. Hearing that he had never returned, the Fat One, redoubled in his worries, went to the bars to greet the two men.

The elder of the two brothers, always looking Manetto directly in the eyes, began by saying, "You have such fine habits, Matteo. You know how many times we have had to deal with your bad ways and how many times we have had to free you from this prison and from others. It is no use to say anything to you, since you always seem to manage to do worse. How we are always in good enough condition to help you, God knows better than man, since you have consumed nearly a fortune. And when will you see little enough value in a thing that you will not spend money on it? Rather, you have thrown money away and wasted it. It goes without saying that everyone can make a joke of you for their amusement. Haven't you half-robbed us? We suffer the pain and also the shame that you don't fear at all. Rather, you do everything in your power to shame your companions. And what do you say when you try to justify your behavior? 'You mistake me for another.' Are you a child? Are you not by now far even from being a youth? But you should be certain of this: if it wasn't for our honor and for the sake of our mother, who is old and sickly and full of sorrow because of you, we would not even think of helping you this time because of all the things you have done to us. But we declare openly this time and for always, that if you ever stumble again, it will be for you to resolve by yourself, and it will be a good deal more trouble than you will ever want to handle. Let this be enough for now." But, being a little besides himself, he added, "So as not to be seen doing these things every day, we will come for you this evening when the Ave Maria rings and when there will be fewer people about, so that not everyone will have to know our miseries and so we won't have too much shame because of your deeds."

The Fat One exchanged a good many words with them. Because they paid his debt and since they both looked him straight in the eye – and it wasn't dark there – it seemed to him, almost without a single doubt, that he had become Matteo.

These brothers said that, for certain, they would no longer have any part in his mistaken ways and that he should never again behave in the manner he had up until then. They also said that if he ever again made similar errors, he would make a joke of himself and of their mother. He strove in every way to convince them that he was Matteo, praying to God that, when the hour approached, they would come for him as they said they would.

The brothers left, and the Fat One turned around and said to the judge, "As if things are not bad enough already, two brothers of Matteo, of this Matteo whom I've become, came here to see me. What can I say?" he asked, looking the judge in the eye. "They have spoken with me face to face and in the light so that they could see if I were someone other than Matteo. After a long admonition they told me that they will come for me at the hour of the Ave Maria and release me from prison." He added, "Until today I would never have believed the things you have told me, but now they are clear to me." Then he said, "So, that worker of yours never returned to who he was before?"

"Never, the poor little man," said the judge.

The Fat One let go of a sigh, and then another one, and then said, "Once I am taken out of here, where will I go and where will I return to? My house will not be mine to return to, but which *is* my house? This is a fine thing. Listen to me," he said, staring at the judge. "If it is the Fat One, whom I am certain I heard with these ears, what can I say that I will not be considered mad or bird-brained? Oh, you know well enough that I will go to that house as if it were mine. By chance the Fat One will be there, and he will say, 'Is he crazy?' If he isn't there, but returns later to find me there, what will happen then? Who will remain there and who will have to go?"

Then the Fat One added, "Oh, you know well that if it were not for this my mother would have done anything in the world to search me out and find me even if I were among the stars. But losing and coming back to oneself, this thing is not well known."

The judge held his laughter with great effort and had inestimable pleasure from this. He said, "Don't go there to your mother, but go with these two who say they are your brothers and see where they lead you and what they do with you. What could you lose in this? First of all, they will pay for you."

"This is the truth," said the Fat One.

The judge continued, "And you will leave prison and have yourself two brothers without a doubt. Who knows, maybe you will do better? Perhaps they are richer than you."

While they spoke of these things it began to get late, and to the judge it seemed like he had to wait a thousand years before he could hurry away from there to laugh, until he couldn't, in any way, wait any longer. Those who pretended to be the brothers of the Fat One were there about in the Mercatánzia always laughing and waiting for it to be time to release him. They saw the case of the judge dispatched, and they saw him leave with dignity, straight-lipped and restrained – trying, as he was, not to burst out in laughter at the Fat One – so that it appeared that he had come to speak with another judge as he had done at other times for clients in legal suits. In this manner they saw him leave.

The brothers, acting as if they had done this many times before, met with the notary and pretended to have reconciled accounts with the creditor and the cashier.

The notary stood up from his seat with the keys of the prison, went to the door and said, "Who is Matteo?"

The Fat One brought himself forward and said, "Here I am, sir," not showing any doubt but that he had become Matteo.

The notary looked at him and said, "These brothers of yours have paid for you and your debts, so that you are free to go." He opened the door of the prison and said, "Come out."

❧

IT WAS VERY DARK when the Fat One was let out of prison, and it seemed to him that it was a good thing to be out of prison without having ever taken money from his own pocket. Because he had gone without eating all that day he wanted to go to his house as soon as he was let out of the prison. But then he remembered that he had heard the Fat One there the night before, so he changed his mind and decided to follow the counsel of the judge and go with these brothers.

Their house was near the church of Santa Felicità at the end of the Costa San Giorgio, and while they were walking there in an easy way, not with the rigidity that they had put on at the prison, they began talking. They informed him of the displeasure he had given their mother, and they reminded him of the promise they had made to him that they would never tolerate this type of behavior from him again. They asked him why he had said he was the Fat One. And they asked him if he was who he seemed to be, or if he actually was the Fat One whom they had taken by mistake and should leave alone.

The Fat One didn't know how to respond to this. He was beside himself and simply went along with them. While half of him confessed to being Matteo, the other half said, 'If I say again that I am the Fat One, perhaps they will want me and not the Fat One, and I will have lost their house as well as my own.'

He promised them that he would never again behave in such a bad way and, to the question about having said that he was the Fat One, he made no response but just stalled for time.

In this way they arrived at the house and the brothers went with him into a ground-floor room, saying to him, "Stay here until it is time for dinner," as if they didn't want to present him to their mother so as not to give her grief.

While he was sitting there beside the fire and near a small table set for dinner, one of the brothers stayed by the fire with him while the other went out to get the priest of Santa Felicità. He was their parish priest and a good person.

The brother said, "I have come to you in confidence since one must go first to those who are close, and because you are my – and our – spiritual Father. So that you will understand everything better and be better able to help us, let me tell you that we are three brothers living close enough to you to be your neighbors, as perhaps you know."

"Yes," said the priest who recognized the brother when he entered.

The brother continued, "One of us is named Matteo. He was held in prison yesterday for his debts. Because this is not the first time that this has happened he has given us all great sorrow, and it appears that he has taken leave of his senses. He appears to be preoccupied about this thing, although in all other ways he is surely the Matteo to whom we are all accustomed. His problem is that he claims to be someone other than Matteo. Have you ever heard a more fantastic thing? He says he has become a certain fat woodworker, an acquaintance of yours no less, who has a shop behind the church of San Giovanni and a house near Santa Maria del Fiore. Even with this man we tried various ways to get this madness out of his head, but it never helped. The reason we have released him from prison and brought him home and put him in a room is so that his madness would not be known to others. As you know, whoever once begins to show these signs and then returns to his senses, is bird-brained. Also, if our mother became aware of this before he returns to his senses, it might cause some inconvenience – how do I know? Women are of weak spirit and she is sickly and old. For these reasons we beg your mercy that you come over to our house. We know that you are a capable man and a good person and that you are astute enough to have discovered the cause of similar problems. For these reasons we wouldn't ask help of anyone other than you. And if you do your best to draw him back from this fantasy we will always be grateful, and later, by God, he will be of some merit. Not to mention that you are responsible for his health since he is in your spiritual care, and you will have to give account. Because if he loses his mind, being in mortal sin, and dies without returning to his senses, he might be damned."

The priest responded that this was the truth and that it was his obligation. He added that, not only did he wish to help him, but that he would make every possible effort. And this was the truth because, other than his obligation, he was servile by nature.

The priest hesitated a bit, and then said, "His problem might be of the type on which my effort would not be lost. Let me be with him for a while… if it isn't dangerous."

"Oh! I understand. You want to know if he is raving mad."

"You know well," said the priest, "people of that type don't have respect for the Father like a priest does, because to them He seems to be something other than what He really is."

"Dear Father, I understand," said the brother. "And you have reason to ask that. But as I have described him to you, he is a person possessed by a pernicious spirit rather than raving mad. Other than you, almost no one would be able to perceive his problem. And truly, if he were raving mad we would give up every hope, and we wouldn't ask anyone's help, because few if any of that type ever return. One may say that he has lost his way a *little,* rather than being totally lost. And we would prefer that our mother not know anything of this. We hope you will let us do it this way."

"If he is as you say he is, I would like to see him,"
responded the priest. "And I will make every effort with
him. Because if he truly is not totally mad, it is everyone's obligation to help him. I know that there is a risk
to your mother, as you say, and one would prefer that
she not have such displeasure, if it is possible."

With this, the brother led the priest to the house and
to the room where the Fat One was.

The Fat One was sitting there with his thoughts, and
when he saw a man enter wearing the habit of a priest,
he stood straight up.

The priest said, "Good evening, Matteo."

The Fat One responded, "Good evening and good
year."

"Now that you say so, it is," said the priest, as it seemed
to him that Matteo was already healed. Then he took
his hand and said, "Matteo, I've come here to be with
you awhile." He drew a small chair near the fire and sat
down next to the Fat One. Seeing that he didn't display
any sign of obstinacy about being the Fat One, as he was
told, he became hopeful and gestured to the brother who
brought him there that things looked well. The brother
indicated that he would wait outside and he left.

The priest started by saying, "You should know this
Matteo: I am your spiritual Father and it is my duty to
counsel all of my people about the spirit and the body as
best I can. I hear that you have been in prison these days
for your debts, and this displeases me enough. But I want
you to understand that this is not something new, nor
should you think that it is. Every day the world gives both
the good and the bad, and one must always be prepared

to have patience. I say this because I abhor the fact that you have given yourself so much sadness that you have almost become crazy. Worthy men don't act this way. But, with the shield of patience and with Providence, they protect themselves from everything as best they can. This is wisdom.

"What foolishness is this I hear – among all the other things you have done and do, which I despise so – that you say you are no longer Matteo, but in every way you wish to be another person named the Fat One who is a woodworker? You are making a bird-brain of yourself with this pertinacity and with your small honor. Truly Matteo, you have much to repent that for such a small adversity you have placed so much grief upon your heart. It seems that you have lost yourself. And for six florins! Oh! Is that such a great debt? Especially now that your brothers have just paid for you?

"My Matteo," said the priest, grasping his hand, "I don't want you to act like this anymore. For the love of me and for your honor and the honor of these two brothers – who appear to be very upright people – promise me that hence forward you will rise from this fantasy and attend to your own business, as upstanding people do and other men who have some sense. Recommend yourself to God, because he who places faith in Him does not do so in vain. It will follow that you will do well, and you will do honor to yourself and to these brothers of yours and to whomever you wish well. And you will do honor to me.

"Why do you do this? Is this Fat One so great a master or so very rich that you wish to be him rather than yourself? What advantage do you see in becoming him?

Let us presume that he is a worthy man and that he might be richer than you, even though your brothers tell me that he is less wealthy than you. If you say that you are him you would not have your own dignity nor your own wealth nor any of the other things that are yours.

"Do as I say, because I am telling you things that you can do to help yourself. Oh, my! If you continue with these infamous ways you will run the risk that your brothers will leave you, among other things, and for this you will be in trouble and loathed for the rest of your life. And this will be what you deserve.

"I promise to report well of you to your brothers, and to make them content. They will love you and help you always as good brothers. Come on Matteo, prepare to be a man, not a beast. Let go of this fantasy. 'Am I the Fat One, or am I not the Fat One?' Do as I say, because I counsel you for the good."

The priest looked him gently in the eye. The Fat One heard with how much love he was told these things. The priest had used very comforting words. At that instant, the Fat One had absolutely no doubt that he was Matteo. He responded to the priest that he was prepared to do as much as he could of what he was told. He told the priest that from that point forward he would make every effort never again to believe himself to be the Fat One, as he had until that point, provided he did not return to being the Fat One. He asked grace from the priest – if it were possible – because he wanted to talk a little longer. While the priest was talking, he surmised it would be an easy thing to escape from this situation because, not having met the Fat One nor spoken to him, he doubted that he had promised anything that would oblige him in the future.

The priest sneered at Matteo's promises and said, "My Matteo, all this is contrary to your deeds, and again I see that you have this confusion in your head. What do you mean, 'Provided that I do not return to being the Fat One?' I don't understand. Do you need to talk with the Fat One? What do you have to do with him? Because the more you speak of this, and the more people you speak to about this, the worse it will be for you. More of this problem will be known and more will be held against you."

Using this argument, the priest tried to convince Matteo that he shouldn't speak with the Fat One and, however unwillingly, Matteo consented.

When he was leaving the priest told the brothers what he said to Matteo, and what Matteo had responded and promised, and that with great difficulty he consented to it all in the end. As for that part of his talk that Matteo did not understand so well, he was not certain if he had truly frightened Matteo into behaving properly, but he had done all that he could. One of the brothers put a large coin in the priest's hand (to make the ploy credible) and they thanked him for his work and asked him to pray to God that He would render their brother healthy. The priest took the coin in his hand and squeezed it. Then he took leave of them and went back to the church.

Filippo di Ser Brunellesco had arrived in the same house where the priest had met Matteo. In another room far away from the Fat One, wearing the largest grin in the world, he was told by one of the brothers of all the things that had happened. He was told of Matteo's release from prison and of all the things he said on his way to the house. The brother also mentioned the judge he saw speaking with the Fat One in prison, and how they saw him leave free. Filippo noted everything well and committed everything to his memory along with everything that the creditor told him.

He gave the brother a small ampule containing a liquid and said, "While you are eating, give this to him to drink – in his wine or in whatever way you like – so long as he is not aware of it. This is an opiate, and there is enough so that he will sleep well, and he will not feel anything for many hours." After he made this accord with the brothers, Filippo went away.

The brothers returned to the room and ate dinner with the Fat One, since by then it was already past three-thirty in the morning. While they were eating they gave him the opiate – which was neither distasteful nor bitter – in such a way that he was unaware of it.

After they ate, they sat around the fire, discussing his bad ways. They begged him for the sake of his soul and for the love of them and the love of their mother that he would be content to be Matteo and abandon this crazy belief that he had become someone else.

They told him that it was too great an error and that he shouldn't marvel at them if they begged this of him because it harmed them as much as it harmed him. They said that the day this thing happened, while they were going to the Mercato Nuova to attend to his debts, one of them heard someone behind them say, "Look at him. He is the forgetful one who has forgotten who he is. He thinks he has become someone else." Although someone else said, "He isn't the one, that is his brother."

While they were discussing this, the opiate began its work so that the Fat One wasn't able to keep his eyes open.

At this one of the brothers said, "It seems you are falling asleep, Matteo. You must have slept very little this past night." This brother spoke the truth.

The Fat One replied, "I swear to you that I have never been so sleepy since the day I was born."

They told him, "Go to your room and go to bed."

With great effort the Fat One got himself to his room, stripped himself and went to bed. He slept deeply because, as Filippo said, he had been given enough opiate so that he didn't hear or feel anything, and he snored like a pig.

❧

AT THE DESIGNATED HOUR, Filippo di Ser Brunellesco returned with six companions – because the Fat One was big and heavy. Among the six were men who had attended the Pecori dinner as well as other witty men who, having heard of this plot – because Filippo informed all of them about everything – wanted to be partisans in this amusement.

They entered the Fat One's bedroom, where he was lying in a deep sleep, and they put him on a stretcher with all of his clothes. They carried him to his house – where, by chance, his mother had not yet returned from the villa, which they knew since they kept a close watch over everything – and they put him in his bed and put his clothes where he usually put them. But since he usually slept with his head at the head of the bed, they left him with his head at the foot of the bed.

Once they did this, they took the key to his shop and went inside. They took all of his hardware and moved it from one place to another. They did the same with his tools, leaving the wood planes with the edges up, and the saws with the teeth down. They did this with all the items in the shop that they could, so that the shop was so mislaid and in such turmoil that it seemed demons had been there. They relocked the shop, returned the key to the Fat One's house, and hung it up by its strap where he usually left it. They left the house, locking the door behind them, and went to their homes and to sleep.

The Fat One slept deeply because of the opiate, and he slept all night without feeling a thing. The next day when the Ave Maria was played from the tower of Santa Maria del Fiore, the opiate had finished its work, and the Fat One woke to a nice morning. He recognized the bells, opened his eyes, and saw a glimpse of the room. He recognized his room, and it quickly cheered his heart, because it seemed to him that he had returned to being the Fat One and in dominion of all the things he thought he had lost. He almost cried for joy, and nearly jumped out of his skin with happiness.

Yet it troubled and surprised him to find himself with his head at the foot of the bed, since he usually slept the other way around. He recalled the things that had happened to him and where he had lain himself down the night before and where he found himself then. He quickly entered into a fantasy of ambiguity. Had he dreamt before, or was he dreaming now? First the one seemed certain to him and then the other.

He looked around the room saying, "This was my room when I was still the Fat One. But when could I have returned here?" He touched himself, first one arm with the opposite hand, then the other arm, and then his chest, affirming with certainty that he was the Fat One.

Then he said to himself, "If this is true, if I am the Fat One, how could I have been mistaken for Matteo? I also remember being in prison, and everyone there knew me as Matteo. Then I was carried off by his two brothers. We went over by Santa Felicità, and a priest spoke with me for a long time. Then I ate, and I went to bed over there, and a deep sleep came over me."

Once again he fell into great confusion over whether he dreamt before or was dreaming now. He began, once again, to feel sad, but not so sad that flashes of happiness couldn't shine through. He remembered what the judge told him in prison, and he figured that he had changed back into the Fat One. He remembered everything that had happened to him until he went to bed the night before; but he didn't worry, since he had returned to being the Fat One, and it seemed to him that he was back on his own two feet.

Then he changed his mind about what had happened, and he repeated to himself, "Who knows if I was dreaming then or if I am dreaming now?" After some deep sighs he said, "God, help me."

He got out of bed as he did in the past, got dressed, and picked up the key to the workshop. He went there, opened the door, and saw everything, each individual object, overturned. Seeing this, while he still had those inextricable doubts, he was assailed by new fears that cancelled all his previous hope, as with a single stroke of a pen. But when the memories of his problem returned, even though he could not persuade himself to be very sure of whether he was doing or dreaming, he returned to the contentment of being back as the Fat One and in possession of his own things.

The two brothers of Matteo arrived at the workshop, and found him seemingly ill at ease. They pretended that they did not know him, and one of them said, "Good day, master."

The Fat One turned around and recognized them. Without responding to their greeting and without having the chance to think about a response he said, "What are you looking for?"

One of them responded, "We have a brother named Matteo who, because he was in prison for a debt and because of some melancholy, has gone a bit out of his mind these past few days. His behavior has caused us some shame, but this is the way he is. Among other things, he claims that he is no longer Matteo, as he is named, but that he is the master of this workshop who, it seems, is called the Fat One. We have tried many times to admonish him and tell him otherwise, but with all the means we've used we haven't been able to rid him of this idiocy, or insolence, as we must call it.

"Last night we brought to him our parish priest from Santa Felicità – which is our parish, and the priest is a good person – and he promised the priest that he would rise from this fantasy. Then he ate dinner with us with the greatest appetite in the world, and he went to bed in our presence. Then, this morning he left the house, leaving the door open so that no one would hear him. Where he went, we do not know. It is for these reasons that we have come here, to see if anything has happened, or if you have heard anything of him."

As the Fat One understood them, these two who earlier had taken him from prison at their expense and had received him in their house to eat and be lodged, no longer knew him as their brother. It seemed to him that all these things proved that he had returned to being the Fat One. Also, seeing them come to his shop, he thought of playfully ridiculing them, as if their shirts did not cover their arses. He said to them, "I would see if he is at the Misericordia Hospital – where lost children are kept – if he is a boy."

The Fat One did not linger with these thoughts because in his hand he had a small wood plane that he had taken to put its iron back in place. Holding the plane like this in one hand – as he had very large hands – he stared them in the face. Because of this, the brothers decided that the Fat One was not in the good mood they expected, and because they were afraid he might beat them, they decided to get out of there quickly and retreat.

The truth is, the Fat One did not have those intentions. Nevertheless, the brothers left. The Fat One could not conceive of how these things had happened. He decided to leave the shop for a little bit and go over to the church of Santa Maria del Fiore, where he could have some peace to think about his troubles and decide better whether he was the Fat One or Matteo by hearing the greetings of the people he encountered on his way.

Once again, because the brothers allowed him to stay at their house but no longer recognized him as Matteo, he was almost certain he was the Fat One. But once again, the ambiguity began to spin in his mind: had he dreamt this or was it true? He moved toward his cloak, which he intended to put on, and then he forgot it and turned toward another corner of the room. Then he returned to it, his mind filled with daydreams.

He began to lose heart. Closing the door behind him, he went toward the church just as he had gone toward his cloak, advancing four steps and turning backward for three. Finally he got hold of his thoughts and said to himself, "This has been a strange case. Let the judge say what he wants, I don't know how this thing could have happened." Then he added, "Since everyone, not just one person, knew me as Matteo, it must certainly have happened."

He tried to draw himself out of these thoughts and to find out only if he had now returned completely to being the Fat One. But this was a mania that was fixed in his mind, and he wondered if he hadn't been transmuted into Matteo again, or even into someone else. With all of these things traversing his mind in one stroke, he needed to understand, to be clear, if things had happened as the judge had told him. He didn't care that going back and forth as he was and being seen there by anyone who might notice him, he might be mistaken for a wounded lion. But since it was a work day there were few people about, and no one was watching him. It seemed to him that this was a good place to vent his feelings to himself.

෴

WHEN HE FINALLY ARRIVED at the church he encountered Filippo and Donatello who were discussing various things, as was their custom. They had arrived at the high point of their vendetta, and they saw him enter.

Filippo knew that the Fat One did not realize that he had been tricked, nor was he suspicious of them. It seemed to them that what they had done, had been done astutely and secretly enough.

Filippo pretended to be happy enough to see him, to dissimulate well, and said, "Things went well enough with my mother. By the time I got to her she had all but recovered, and so I didn't send for you. She has had these accidents before. Old people do these sorts of things. I didn't see you afterwards. What happened to you last night? Have you heard this story of Matteo Mannini?"

The Fat One became unhinged, and he didn't turn to face either Donatello or Filippo.

"What happened?" asked Donatello.

Filippo responded, "You don't know?" Turning toward the Fat One he said, "It seems that the night we were together, between two and three o'clock, he was around here in the piazza. There were guards and messengers with him who were taking him away. I don't know who they were but this doesn't matter. And he said to them and also to his family, 'What do you want with me? You have taken me by mistake. I don't have any debts with anyone. I am the Fat One, the woodworker. Do you want *me?*'"

To the Fat One, what Filippo was saying didn't seem suspicious, and it seemed natural enough that he would know these things.

Filippo continued, "The person who ordered him taken approached him and said, 'Look at what you will try to get away with. We will get the better of you. If we don't do this now you will waste all your money. And we must be paid. You can't blame us if we argue when we don't get paid.'

"The one who had him taken was a collector for a creditor, and he went up to him and with a fixed look said, 'He is pretending to be someone else, the rogue!' Then he looked at him very, very well, and said, 'He certainly is Matteo. Take him away and lock him up well this time.' While they were taking him away he said again and again that he was the Fat One, the woodworker, and he tried to prove it by saying, 'Look, I have just locked up the workshop,' while showing them a key."

This was exactly as things happened, as Filippo had been told by the young messenger. He continued, "I heard that there was a party in the Mercatánzia at exactly the same time. Could it be that you've heard nothing of this?" he asked, wearing the largest smile in the world.

Donatello also pretended that he had heard nothing of this. He said, "I remember that just yesterday something was said about this at my workshop, but I was busy and preoccupied and I didn't listen well. But I heard – now that I remember – the names 'Matteo' and the 'Fat One' as well as the words 'taken away', but I didn't think to ask about it because I wasn't thinking about the Fat One. Beh, tell me Filippo, what happened here – since you know about it? Oh, this is certainly something to laugh about: that is, that he was taken away and he didn't want to be Matteo. How could this happen?"

Filippo said, "Oh, it can't be that the Fat One doesn't know. What happened to you yesterday? Could it be that you didn't go to your workshop? Once I heard this story I made ten circles of Florence to find you and tell you this. I went to your shop three or four times to explain this to you. I waited for you there but you never came."

The Fat One looked now at Filippo, now at Donatello, and he wanted to respond first to the one and then to the other. But he cut off his words, trying to express first one thing and then another, so that his words had no meaning and he seemed like a man possessed. It was impossible to tell whether he was a bird-brain or he was speaking the truth.

After a deep sigh he said, "Filippo, this is news to me!"

Filippo went quickly to what he wanted to say, holding back a smirk with great effort. "You tell me that you've heard nothing of this? How could this be?" He pulled up a chair so that he could sit and be more at ease while he listened.

The Fat One regretted having said these words, and he didn't know what to do. He was completely embarrassed because he knew when they were discussing something seriously (as they were now) and when they were not.

Just at that moment, Matteo arrived, unexpectedly and without warning – he was also part of the vendetta, all arranged by Filippo.

"Fortunes help us, Matteo, you could not have arrived at a better time" Filippo said, greeting him.

The Fat One turned toward him, absolutely lost, and managed to say, "Your brothers were just at my workshop looking for you." Then he restrained himself.

Filippo said, "Where have you come from, Matteo? We have heard some things about you, and we were just talking about you – everyone is right now."

Donatello asked Matteo, "Have you been put in prison one of these past nights? Tell the truth, because Filippo tells me…"

"Is no one put in prison anymore?" asked Matteo. Then he said to Filippo, who was staring at him, "I have come from my home."

"Oh," said Filippo. "And I heard you were taken to prison."

"Fine. I was taken to prison. I was paid for. I was let out. I am here. What the devil is this? Don't you have anything to talk about anymore but my problems? All morning my mother swamped me with questions from the moment I got home. And those brothers of mine were harsh with me, looking at me as if I had grown horns since I returned from my villa. As soon as they found me there, they demanded, 'What time did you leave this morning and leave the door open?' It appeared to me that they had gone crazy along with my mother. I don't understand it. Then they said, I don't know –

something about my being arrested and that they paid for me. Crazy, in a word."

Filippo said, "Where have you been? I haven't seen you for many days."

Matteo said, "I will tell you the very truth, Filippo. It is true that I had a debt in good faith with a store for six florins. I held this debt on my word of honor because I was also owed a debt of eight florins by a person from Empoli. According to what was last promised to me, I should have had that money many days ago, so I designated this money for my debt and my creditor advanced me those six florins. I promised my creditor on Saturday that I would pay him Tuesday, so that he would never lack for anything, as he also promised me. He had a judgment of the Magistrate in his favor (because truly it was a long time that I owed him, since I was hard up for money) so I made the decision to go away from here to our place at Certosa, so that I would not seem uncivil. I was there for two days. You haven't seen me because it hasn't been an hour since I've returned. While I was there, something happened to me that is the most remarkable thing that you've ever heard.

"I went away to the villa on Tuesday after dinner because I had no business and because it has been a thousand years since I have been there. There is nothing there but one bed, since all we do there is let the wines come to vintage, as every other thing, in its own time. I went there, idling along the way to waste time, and I had a couple of drinks along the way in Galluzzo so that I wouldn't trouble our worker at the villa about dinner. I arrived at the villa at night, and I asked the worker to light a lamp for me and went away to bed. What I will tell you now is something to laugh about. Every bit of it seems crazy to me, but I will say it anyway, and I am perhaps crazier than all of this.

"I dressed myself this morning at the villa and opened a window. I will tell you the truth – I don't know if I am dreaming right now or if I dreamt what I will tell you. It seemed to me that I was someone other than myself this morning. This is something to laugh about, Filippo. Now let me continue.

"My worker who gave me the lamp said to me this morning, 'What happened to you yesterday?' I said, 'Didn't you see me last night?' He said, 'Not I, when?' I said, 'Forgetful! Didn't you light the oil lamp for me, as you know it wasn't burning?' He said, 'Yes, the night before. But last night I didn't see you, nor all day yesterday. I thought you went to Florence, and I was amazed that you hadn't said anything to me. I thought you went there for some business.'

"Therefore, I slept all day yesterday. And I asked the worker, 'What day is today?' He told me that it was Thursday. In effect, Filippo, I find that I have slept for one entire day and two entire nights without ever stirring. I have only slept."

Filippo and Donatello made faces of amazement and sat listening with attention. Filippo said, "What you ate must have been well digested."

Matteo said, "I am only telling you what happened."

"It wouldn't be a good idea to wait to eat dinner with you," said Donatello.

This story of having slept all this time was amazing to the Fat One, and he said to himself, "There is no remedy for me. I must certainly be insane. I would never have believed this story three days ago, and yet I am…"

Matteo continued his speech, "I dreamt the craziest things that have ever been heard."

Said Filippo, "The empty head is like that. It needs to eat."

"I just encountered," continued Matteo, "an apprentice of the store to which I owed those six florins. He asked me to excuse him and said that it wasn't he who had me taken to prison. And he said, 'You apologize now for your many expenses and for how much they have added up, but from what I can see, they have been paid.'" With these words from the apprentice, I began to understand the scoldings of my mother and my brothers, who seemed crazy to me. As I just now told you, they paid for my debt, but how, I don't yet know. I wanted this apprentice to explain, and, in effect, I found that all of this happened during the time I believed I was asleep. It seems that I spent the greater part of that time in prison. Filippo, explain this to me, because I don't know how this could possibly have happened. It seems that I've waited a thousand years to see you and tell this to you and laugh about this with you."

Then Matteo turned toward the Fat One and said, "I have spent the better part of this time between your house and your workshop. I have to laugh about this. I find that someone has paid a debt for me of many florins while I have slept. And while I slept I thought myself to be another person. Oh, it is as certain as I find myself here among you now. But who knows if I am dreaming now or if I was dreaming then."

Donatello said, "I don't understand you. Tell me again. I thought you said something else. Oh, you are making me go crazy. You just now said that you were at your villa."

Matteo said, "You understood me well."

Filippo said, "He wanted to say he was dreaming."

Then Matteo said, "Filippo understood me."

The Fat One didn't say a word. He was like a person possessed, and he listened very attentively to understand if he was Matteo during that time. Filippo was like a scratching piglet. Every so often, one of them would break away and go to the choir of the church when he could not help but laugh a little at the transfixed Fat One.

Filippo took the hand of the Fat One and said, "Let us all gather together in the choir and don't anyone go away, since this is one of the best stories I have ever heard in my days, and I want to understand it well. Tell me more of this story Matteo, and you will hear it from me again in another place and time, because it will be retold throughout the land. The rest of this story beckons because it is not yet complete."

They all sat down in one corner of the choir so that they could see one another easily. The choir was, in those times, between two large columns in the front as one entered the tribune. They sat there awhile not saying anything because Filippo waited for Matteo to start speaking while Matteo was waiting for Filippo to start.

Filippo spoke first, and he turned more toward Matteo – who was playing his part well – than toward the Fat One – who was not yet broken – and said, while laughing, "You hear what is being said around Florence. I have just now told you all as it was told to me, and you will hear it again since you want me to be the one to speak first. It is said that Tuesday night you were held in prison."

"Me held?" said Matteo.

"Yes," said Filippo. "For your debt. What do you say about that?" Turning toward Donatello he said, "You see, something has happened."

Donatello asked Matteo, "And where were you when I found you knocking on the door of the Fat One's house the other night?"

Matteo said, "When? I don't know if I would ever knock on his door."

"You never knocked on his door?" said Donatello. "Didn't you speak with me at his door?"

Matteo made an expression of pure amazement.

Filippo continued with Matteo, "While you were being dragged away to prison, you said first to the messenger and then to those who held you, 'You have taken me by mistake. You have seized me by mistake. You don't want me.' And you defended yourself as much as you could by saying that you were the Fat One here. Now, you say you were in your villa and, according to what you declare and what we hear, you were in bed asleep."

"Say what you will," said Matteo, "but you mock me. I was at the villa as I have told you, so as not to be arrested, since that was something I truly feared. And as to what

Donatello just said, I would swear on a consecrated altar that I would not now nor would I ever knock on the door of the Fat One's house. You must understand that these things that have happened are so very strange.

"I sent my friend, who lives in Palagio, to a notary to get a legal pass for me so that I would not be arrested for my debt. He had it sent to me at the villa, and until yesterday he believed that I had it. The notary wrote me a note early this morning and sent a messenger to give it to me. The note said that the magistrates had not convened but were away in their villas. Since they had no other important business, those gentlemen did not want to return just to write passes. He added that I should stay at the villa for a few days and wait for the pass. Yet, I did return, under cover, but since I have been paid for, everything is fine. Filippo, Donatello, this is the very truth.

"But the dreams I had during that time are truly something to laugh about, Filippo. I am not teasing. I don't think I ever dreamt so, the dreams seemed so real. I seemed to be in his house," he said, touching the Fat One. "And it seemed that his mother was my mother. I spoke comfortably with her, as if she were my own mother, and I ate with her and talked of my business to her, and she answered me. I remember a thousand things she said to me. I went to bed in that house, and I woke up and went to the workshop of the woodworker. It seemed to me that I wanted to work, as I have seen the Fat One work a thousand times before when I visited him in his shop. It didn't seem to me that there was a single tool in the shop that was in good order, so I fixed them all."

The Fat One looked on as if crazed. Even then he had tools in his hands.

Matteo continued, "I tried to work with them but they didn't serve me. They all worked the same way so I decided to put them anywhere other than where they used to be, keeping in mind where they were so that I could put them back when I had the time. I took the others away, and I handled all of them in one way or another. It occurred to me to answer anyone who came by to ask of things as if I were really him. It seemed to work. I went out to eat, and at night I locked up the shop and went home to bed. The house seemed to me to be truly as it is and as I have seen it. So, truly, here you are with the Fat One, as you know."

The Fat One sat dumbstruck for an hour because he didn't think it was worthwhile to say anything in front of Filippo who knew and saw everything, down to the hair on the egg. But hearing this dream took away every doubt from the Fat One, who could not be better tied in one inextricable tangle. To hear this dream of one day and two nights seemed to him to take as long as all the time of his troubles.

Filippo and Donatello expressed the greatest wonder in the world at hearing this dream. Then Filippo said, "From this it would seem that neither you nor Matteo were arrested. And you say as well that you were paid for and that you were at your villa. This is a knot that even Aristotle would not be able to untangle."

The Fat One, thinking of what Matteo had said – that he thought he was the Fat One – and remembering what the judge had told him in prison, decided to speak.

Pressing his lips together and leaning his head forward he said, "Filippo, these are strange things, but I hear that these things have happened before. Matteo has spoken and you all have spoken and I would also like to speak, but I would, perhaps, say too many things for which you would hold me crazy. I need to keep quiet. Filippo, oh, don't discuss this anymore."

It seemed to the Fat One that the judge had clearly told him the truth. Since what had happened to him fit exactly with Matteo's dream it seemed certain that he had been Matteo at that time, and Matteo had been him. And the Fat One thought that since Matteo had been sleeping, he was less tormented by what had happened, and it wasn't as important to him, nor as troubling. It also seemed certain to him that he had returned to being the Fat One since he heard the story of Matteo and saw that Matteo was no longer the Fat One.

The Fat One's mother had not yet returned from their villa in Polverosa. It seemed to him that he would have to wait a thousand years to see her and ask her if she had been in Florence these past days, and ask who had knocked at her door, who was in the house with her, and who had opened the workshop during that time.

He took leave of them. They didn't try to hold him back with anything other than light and courteous pressure because he hadn't yet taken offence, and because they wanted to give vent to their laughter, which they couldn't hold back any longer. Filippo said, "It would be nice if we could dine together one night." At this point the Fat One left without responding.

ONE CANNOT BE SURPRISED if Donatello and Filippo laughed so much. Anyone who saw them or heard them would think them more crazed than the Fat One. Donatello and Filippo carried on without restraint. Filippo laughed uproariously, looking from one person to the next.

The Fat One decided to go to Polverosa to find out for himself what had happened. He found his mother there and learned that she had not been in Florence in those days, and she told him the reason she was delayed. Because of this, while thinking and rethinking about what had happened to him and how he returned to himself, he concluded that it must have been a prank. He did not yet understand, however, the reason why. But it appeared to him to be just so, because his mother was not in Florence and his house was empty during that time. As much as he tried he could not find a reason for what happened, and he didn't have the heart to defend himself from being put in such mockery and from being so deceived. But mostly it bothered him that Filippo had taken such an interest in this, and it didn't seem possible to him for Filippo to make amends.

For these reasons he decided to go to Hungary, where he had once been invited. The person who invited him had been his friend and companion when they both worked in the intarsia shop of Maestro Pellegrino in Via Terma. This friend had gone to Hungary many years back and had done very well there with the help of Filippo Scolary, who is called the Spano.

This Spano, a citizen of Florence, was Captain General in the army of Sigismund, the king of Hungary, and the son of King Charles of Bohemia. Sigismund was a very wise and cunning king who was elected emperor in the time of Gregory XII, and he was crowned Caesar by Pope Eugenio IV. The Spano had compassion for all the Florentines he came across, whether they had intellectual or manual skills, because he was a very upright man who loved the nation as much as the nation loved him. And he did good things for many people.

In the past few days, the Fat One's companion had come to Florence to see if he could bring but one master of the Fat One's art to Hungary, because he had so much work that had to be done immediately. He discussed this many times with the Fat One, begging him to come to Hungary and showing him that in a short time he could make riches for himself.

After he returned to Florence, the Fat One ran into his companion, and because of what had been done to him he said, "You have tried many times to convince me to go with you to Hungary, and I have always said 'No.' Now, by chance, a certain problem has occurred with my mother, and I have decided to go, if you still want me. If you do, I must leave tomorrow morning, because if I stay longer I will not be able to leave."

His friend replied that it would be very costly to him to leave the next morning because he had not yet finished all of his business, but if the Fat One needed to leave Florence he should go to Bologna and wait for him, and he would meet him there in a few days.

The Fat One and his friend agreed upon this and the Fat One left feeling content. He returned to his shop and took some tools and trifles to bring along and took any money that he had. He left a letter in his house addressed to his mother that said he guaranteed her, as an endowment, what was left in the shop, and that he had gone to Hungary with the intention of staying for many years. When he had done this he went to Borgo San Lorenzo to wait for a coach going to Bologna, without saying a word to his family or anyone else, as if he were game and had hunters behind him.

He went around Florence on horseback to see what little he could of the city in the brief time that remained, and he dismounted in some places where he heard his case being discussed, each person laughing and making jokes about it. In this way he heard from someone that it had been a prank. He also heard what he had said to the men who arrested him and to the judge he spoke with in prison, because the judge met with Filippo and recounted all that had been said. When he learned that it had been a joke, the judge had the greatest laugh of all.

It was generally said around Florence that the prank had been played on him by Filippo di Ser Brunellesco, and this very much convinced the Fat One because he knew Filippo all too well. Realizing that he was being scoffed at, he knew that it must have started with Filippo. All these reasons gave him great comfort in his decision to leave. In this way he left Florence, and when he met his companion in Bologna, they went to Hungary.

⌒

THE GROUP FROM THAT DINNER met again, as it was their custom to meet from time to time. The first time they gathered together again it was in the same place, in the house of Tomaso Pecori. They met so they could talk about the prank and laugh about it all together. They invited the judge who was with the Fat One in prison. He accepted happily because he wanted to meet and know everyone, and to hear every detail about the prank, and he knew that they wanted the same. They asked the young messenger to come, as well as Matteo and those two brothers who led him from prison to their home and hearth. They wanted the notary at the prison to attend, but he was not able to come.

The judge heard with great pleasure how the prank grew. He told them about the Fat One's questions and how he replied to them by speaking of Apuleius, Circe, and Actaeon, and of his worker, to make things seem more realistic. He also said that if anything else had occurred to him, he would have told him.

They had the greatest amusement from this, jumping from one instance to another according to what they recalled. Seeing how things had happened, with the judge and with the priest and everything in general, they knew how much Fortune had helped them. The judge said that he never remembered, in all the times of his life, being at a banquet where he had eaten better food or had greater quantities of it. He said that he had never had such a good time at the tables of kings and emperors, as he did at those of minor princes and private men such as they were. And there was no one who could say that he could have defended himself better than the Fat One had the joke been played upon him, such was the caution and planning of Filippo.

∾

ONCE THE FAT ONE and his companion arrived in Hungary, they gave themselves over to their work and they met with good fortune. In a few years they became rich, considering their rank, thanks to the Spano. He made the Fat One a master engineer and called him Maestro Manetto da Firenze. The Fat One had a good reputation with everyone, and the Spano took him to the field with him when he went on military exercises. He received good commissions, sometimes by rich and beautiful women who, by chance, had need of him.

The Spano was as liberal and magnanimous as if he were born of a king. He was this way toward everyone, but especially toward the Florentines, who came to Hungary happily, knowing that he would support and favor them. The Fat One could do his every bidding, and he worked with his companion when he was not working in the field.

The Fat One returned to Florence more often and for longer periods of time as the years passed. On his first return he asked Filippo the reason for this game in Florence. Quickly, and without conferring with his friends, Filippo told him this story. The Fat One smiled while hearing this story. He smiled at the thousand wonderful things within the story and within himself.

He smiled at his confusion about whether he was or was not the Fat One, and whether he was dreaming or remembering dreams when he thought of the past. And he smiled about things that no one else knew about.

Filippo never before laughed about these things with such good heart as he did this time. The Fat One looked him in the eye and said, "You know better than I, that I am much scoffed at in Santa Maria del Fiore."

Filippo said, "Let them do so. This will give you more fame than anything you have ever done with the Spano or Sigismund. People will be talking about you for a hundred years." Filippo laughed, and so did the Fat One, no less so this time.

As time went on, the Fat One was never found to be with anyone other than Filippo, even though he was certain that Filippo was the instigator of everything. Filippo teased him whenever he was with him saying, "I knew at that time that I had to do this to you in order to make you rich. There are very many people who wanted very much to have been the Fat One, and to have had these jokes played upon them. You have become rich, you and your family and friends, by the graces of the emperor of the world, and the Spano, and many other great princes and barons."

These comings and goings of the Fat One gave him opportunities to meet with Filippo and examine the prank; to mince every particular detail given by the judge or the messenger or the others. The funniest things about the prank remained, it was said, in the mind of the Fat One.

From these meetings arose the idea that the story could be kept more complete and with more minute detail if it were written down. Filippo repeated the story again, sometimes with great detail, and those who heard it passed it on to others. But, whoever heard it from him affirms that it is impossible to give every detail as to how the story went, so that many pleasing parts that Filippo recalled and that were true do not survive. After Filippo died, it was recalled by some who heard it many times from him, such as the one called Antonio di Matteo dalle Porte, by Michelozzo, by Andreino da San Gemignano who was his disciple, by the Scheggia, by Feo Belcari, by Luca della Robbia, by Antonio di Migliore Guidoti, by Domenico di Michelino, and by many others.

Although the person who first wrote this might have found something written in his time, it could not have been a third of the event, and in many places it must have been fragmented and full of mends. And perhaps he has done well in writing this, so that it would not be wholly lost.

Thanks be to God. Amen. ✿✿✿

GLOSSARY

Actaeon – A mythological hunter transformed by Diana into a stag as punishment for having come upon the goddess in her bath. He was then torn to pieces by his own hounds.

Apuleuis (born c.123 AD) – Lucius Apuleius was a Roman writer whose best known work is a humorous fable called *The Golden Ass*. In it the main character is changed from a man into a beast by the Goddess Isis. He lives twelve months as an ass before being changed back into a man. The story con-tains the mystical lessons of regeneration and transmutation.

Belcari, Feo (1410-1484) – Author of some of the earliest known devotional works in Italian, including *Vita del Beato Colombini and Sacra rappresentazione di Abraham e di Isaac suo figliuolo.*

Brunellesco, Filippo di Ser (1377-1446) – Florentine architect and sculptor – his paintings do not survive – inventor of linear perspective. Using extraordinary technical skill Brunelleschi designed and built the dome that crowns the cathedral of Santa Maria del Fiore (Il Duomo) in Florence. *See introduction.*

Certosa – Area surrounding the Certosa monastery in Galluzzo.

Charles of Bohemia, king (1346-1378) – Called Charles IV, emperor and king of Bohemia. He founded the University of Prague in 1347. He was the father of both Sigismund, king of Hungary, and Wencelas, king of Bohemia.

Circe – Mythological enchantress who lived on the island of Aeaea in Greece. She transformed men who drank from her cup into pigs.

Dalle Porte, Antonio Di Matteo (1427-1479) – True name Antonio Gamberelli, called Il Rossellino. Florentine sculp-tor whose most important work is the tomb of the cardinal of Portugal in the church of San Miniato al Monte.

Della Robbia, Luca (1400-1482) – Florentine sculptor who carved the marble reliefs for the Singer's Pulpit in the cathedral of Santa Maria del Fiore. He is well-known for his blue and white glazed terracotta relief sculptures found throughout the churches of Florence.

Donatello (1386-1466) – Sculptor and architect, a devoted friend of Brunelleschi, and an expert in perspective whose graceful masterpieces adorn many corners of Florence. One of his most famous works is his youthful and suggestive statue of David.

Eugenio IV, pope (1383-1447) – Born in Venice to a wealthy merchant family, he resided in Florence as pope in the 1430s and formally consecrated the cathedral of Florence.

Florin – Florentine gold coin with lily stamped on one side and figure of St. John stamped on the other.

Fortune – Roman goddess of destiny, fate, and that which "turns" the cycle of the year like a wheel. Hence, the expression "wheel of Fortune."

Galluzzo – Small town located to the south of Florence. A monastic citadel built in 1341 called Certosa del Galluzzo is located there.

Gregory XII, pope (1323-1417) – Venetian elected to the Roman papacy in 1406 during the Great Schism. The Council of Pisa was called in 1409 to reconcile the schism by having both Pope Gregory and the Avignon Pope Benedict abdicate simultaneously. When they refused the council deposed both Gregory and Benedict and elected Alexander V. However, neither Gregory nor Benedict recognized the authority of the council and the result was a divided Church with three popes. Alexander V's successor, John XXIII (Baldassare Cossa) was later deposed on charges of murder, rape, sodomy, incest and piracy. Cossa's tomb in the Florentine Baptistry was commissioned by Cosimo de' Medici and designed by Donatello and Michelozzo.

Judge, the – Possibly the historical figure Giovanni Gherardi da Prato, a learned man who never kept track of his debts.

Mercatánzia – The mercantile court that had supreme jurisdiction over disputes arising from mercantile activity. It was located near the church of Orsanmichele in Florence.

Glossary

Mercato Nuovo – The open marketplace near the Piazza Signoria in the center of the old city of Florence.

Michelino, Domenico di (1417-1491) – True name Domenico di Francesco, painter and disciple of Beato Angelico.

Michelozzo (1396-1472) – Full name Michelozzo di Bartolomeo, Florentine sculptor, architect, student of Donatello and friend and follower of Brunelleschi. His best known work is the Palazzo Medici-Riccardi, which he designed for Cosimo de' Medici.

Misericordia – The confraternity located at the Piazza San Giovanni at the corner of Via dei Calzaiuoli. Dedicated to works of charity, the brothers once sheltered lost and abandoned children.

Pecori, Tomaso – A member of the Pecori family whose houses were near Piazza San Giovanni. There is now a street on the southwest corner of the Piazza called Via de' Pecori. In a later version of *The Fat Woodworker* by Bernardo Giambullari, Pier Pecori (Piero di Bartolommeo di Iacopo Pecori) takes the place of Tomaso. Pier was a prior and later gonfalonier who died in 1465.

Polverosa – Town on the outskirts of Florence where many prominent Florentines owned land.

Rucellai, Giovanni di Messer Francesco – Member of a wealthy and politically prominent Florentine family who made their fortune in the wool trade. As patrons of the arts the Rucellai commissioned such works as the chapel of San Sepolcro and the facade of Santa Maria Novella.

San Gemignano, Andreino da (1412-1462) – True name Andrea Cavalcanti, born at Borgo a Buggiano and called Il Buggiano, here misnamed da San Gemignano by Manetti. A minor sculptor and architect who worked with Brunelleschi, Luca della Robbia, Donatello, and others, he was orphaned because of war and adopted by Brunelleschi at age 5. Although devoted to his adoptive father, he once stole jewels and 200 florins from Brunelleschi and fled to Naples. The reconciliation required the intervention of Pope Eugenio IV.

San Giorgio, Costa di – Street located on the Oltrarno in Florence, which begins near the church of Santa Felicità and runs around Fort Belvedere behind the Pitti Palace.

San Giovanni, church of – Florentine Baptistry dating from the year 1000, said to be constructed over the site of a former Roman temple to Mars. This eight-sided building faced with green and white marble was the first cathedral of Florence. Its three enormous bronze doors are carved in relief by Ghiberti with stories from the Bible. The east doors were referred to as "the Gates of Paradise" by Michelangelo.

San Lorenzo, Borgo – Street which runs north from the Piazza San Giovanni to Piazza San Lorenzo, site of the church of San Lorenzo.

Santa Felicità, church of – Church located on the Oltrarno near the Ponte Vecchio. It was built on the site of a fifth century cemetery and is connected to the Pitti Palace and the Palazzo Vecchio by covered passages. It contains the Capponi Chapel designed by Brunelleschi.

Santa Maria del Fiore – The cathedral of Florence, also called the Duomo, begun by Arnolfo di Cambio in 1294. Brunelleschi erected its celebrated dome in 1420.

Scheggia, the – (1407-1486) Giovanni di Ser Giovanni Guidi called La Scheggia. Artist and brother of the famed Masaccio.

Sigismund, king of Hungary (1410-1437) – An ally of Florence whose emblem is inserted on one of the reliefs inside the cathedral of Santa Maria del Fiore.

Spano, the (1369-1426) – Filippo Buondelmonte Scolari, called the Spano. An Italian condottiero who was made governor general of Hungary by Sigismund, and count of Temesvar di Ispani – hence the name "Spano."

Via Terma – A street in Florence so named because it was the site in ancient times of the public baths. Near the Mercato Nuovo, it was lined with silk workshops in the fifteenth cen-tury. One side of the Parte Guelfa Palace faced the street. The facade of the palace was designed by Brunelleschi.

Ulysses (Greek: Odysseus) – Mythological hero of Homer's Odyssey who wanders for ten adventurous years before returning to his homeland of Ithaca. Hero of the Trojan War, he invented the trick of the Trojan Horse.

BIBLIOGRAPHY

Apuleius, Lucius. *The Golden Ass.* Trans. Robert Graves. New York: Penguin, 1950.

Baron, Hans. *The Crisis of the Early Italian Renaissance.* Princeton: Princeton University Press, 1966.

Battisti, Eugenio. *Filippo Brunelleschi, The Complete Work.* Trans. Robert Erich Wolf. New York: Rizzoli, 1981.

Benivieni, Girolamo. "Dialogo di Antonio Manetti Cittadino Fiorentino Circa al Sito, Forma e Misura dello Inferno di Dante," in *Studi sulla Divina Commedia di Galileo Galilei, Vincenzo Borghini, et altri.* Ed. Ottavio Gigli, 37-135. Florence: Le Monnier, 1855.

Boccaccio, Giovanni. *The Decameron.* Trans. Mark Musa and Peter Bondanella. New York: Mentor, 1982.

Brucker, Gene A. *Renaissance Florence.* New York: John Wiley, 1969.

—. *The Society of Renaissance Florence: A Documentary Study.* New York: Harper & Row, 1971.

Burckhardt, Jacob. *The Civilization of the Renaissance in Italy.* Trans. S. G. C. Middlemore. Oxford & London: Phaidon Press, 1945.

Cavalcanti, Guido. *The Complete Poems.* Ed. & trans. Marc Cirigliano. New York: Italica Press, 1992.

Chaucer, Geoffrey. *The Complete Works of Geoffrey Chaucer.* Ed. F. N. Robinson. 2d ed. New York: Oxford University Press, 1957.

Dionisotti, Carlo. "Antonio Manetti Copista" in Edite e rari: *Studi sulla tradizione letteraria tra tre e cinque cento.* Ed. Domenico De Robertis, 183-231. Milan: Feltrinelli, 1978.

Edgerton, Samuel Y., Jr. *The Renaissance Rediscovery of Linear Perspective.* New York: Harper & Row, 1976.

Firenzuola, Agnolo. *Tales of Firenzuola.* New York: Italica Press, 1987.

Bibliography

Gadol, Joan. *Leon Battista Alberti: Universal Man of the Early Renaissance.* Chicago: University of Chicago Press, 1973.

Giambullari, Bernardo. "La Novella del Grasso Legnaiuolo" in *Rime inedite o rare di Bernardo Giambullari.* Ed. Italiano Marchetti, 91-139. Florence: Sansoni Antiquariato, 1955.

Hay, Denys and John Law. *Italy in the Age of the Renaissance, 1380-1530.* London and New York: Longman, 1989.

Ivins, William M., Jr. *Art & Geometry: A Study in Space Intuitions.* New York: Dover, 1964.

———. *On the Rationalization of Sight.* New York: Da Capo Press, 1973.

Kemp, Martin. *The Science of Art.* New Haven, CT: Yale University Press, 1990.

Krautheimer, Richard, with Trude Krautheimer-Hess. *Lorenzo Ghiberti.* Princeton: Princeton University Press, 1982.

Kristeller, Paul Oskar. *Renaissance Thought.* New York: Harper & Row, 1961.

———. *Renaissance Thought & the Arts.* Princeton: Princeton University Press, 1990.

Kubovy, Michael. *The Psychology of Perspective and Renaissance Art.* New York: Cambridge University Press, 1989.

Manetti, Antonio. "La Novella del Grasso Legnaiuolo," in *Collezione di classici italiani.* Series 2. Ed. Giuseppe Morpurgo, 43:101-46. Turin: Unione Tipographico-Editrice Torinese, 1926.

Manetti, Antonio Di Tuccio. *The Life of Brunelleschi.* Ed. Howard Saalman. Trans. Catherine Enggass. University Park, PA: Pennsylvania State University Press, 1979.

Martines, Lauro. *Power and Imagination: City-States in Renaissance Italy.* New York: Vintage, 1979.

———. *The Social World of the Italian Humanists, 1390-1460.* Princeton: Princeton University Press, 1963.

McCarthy, Mary. *The Stones of Florence.* New York: Harcourt Brace Jovanovich, 1963.

Medici, Lorenzo De' (Il Magnifico). *Tutti le opere: Scritti giocosi.* Ed. Gigi Cavalli. Milan: Rizzoli, 1958.

Murray, Peter. *The Architecture of the Italian Renaissance.* New York: Schocken, 1976.

Tartaro, Achille. "La Letteratura volgare in Toscana," in *La letteratura italiana, Il Quattrocento* 3 (no. 1): 198-225. Bari: Laterza, 1971.

Schevill, Ferdinand. *Medieval and Renaissance Florence.* 2 vols. New York: Harper & Row, 1963.

Uzielli, G. "Antonio di Tuccio Manetti, Paolo Toscanelli e la lunghezza delle miglia nel secolo delle scoperte." *Rivista geografica italiana* 9 (1902): 473-98.

Vasari, Giorgio. *The Lives of the Artists.* Abridged. Trans. George Bull. New York: Penguin, 1982.

Vespasiano da Bisticci. *Renaissance Princes, Popes & Prelates.* Trans. William George & Emily Waters. Intro. by Myron P. Gilmore. New York: Harper & Row, 1963.

Vitruvius Pollio, Marcus. *The Ten Books on Architecture.* Trans. Morris Hicky Morgan. New York: Dover, 1960.

Wackernagel, M. *The World of the Florentine Artist.* Princeton: Princeton University Press, 1981.

White, John. *The Birth & Rebirth of Pictoral Space.* Cambridge, MA: Harvard University Press, 1987.

Wind, Edgar. Pagan *Mysteries in the Renaissance.* New York: Oxford University Press, 1980.

*This Book Was Completed on October 24, 2000
at Italica Press, New York, New York
& Was Set in Galliard & Granjon.
It Was Printed On 60-lb
Natural Paper
by BookSurge
U. S. A./
E. U.
* *
**

Made in the USA
Monee, IL
04 August 2023